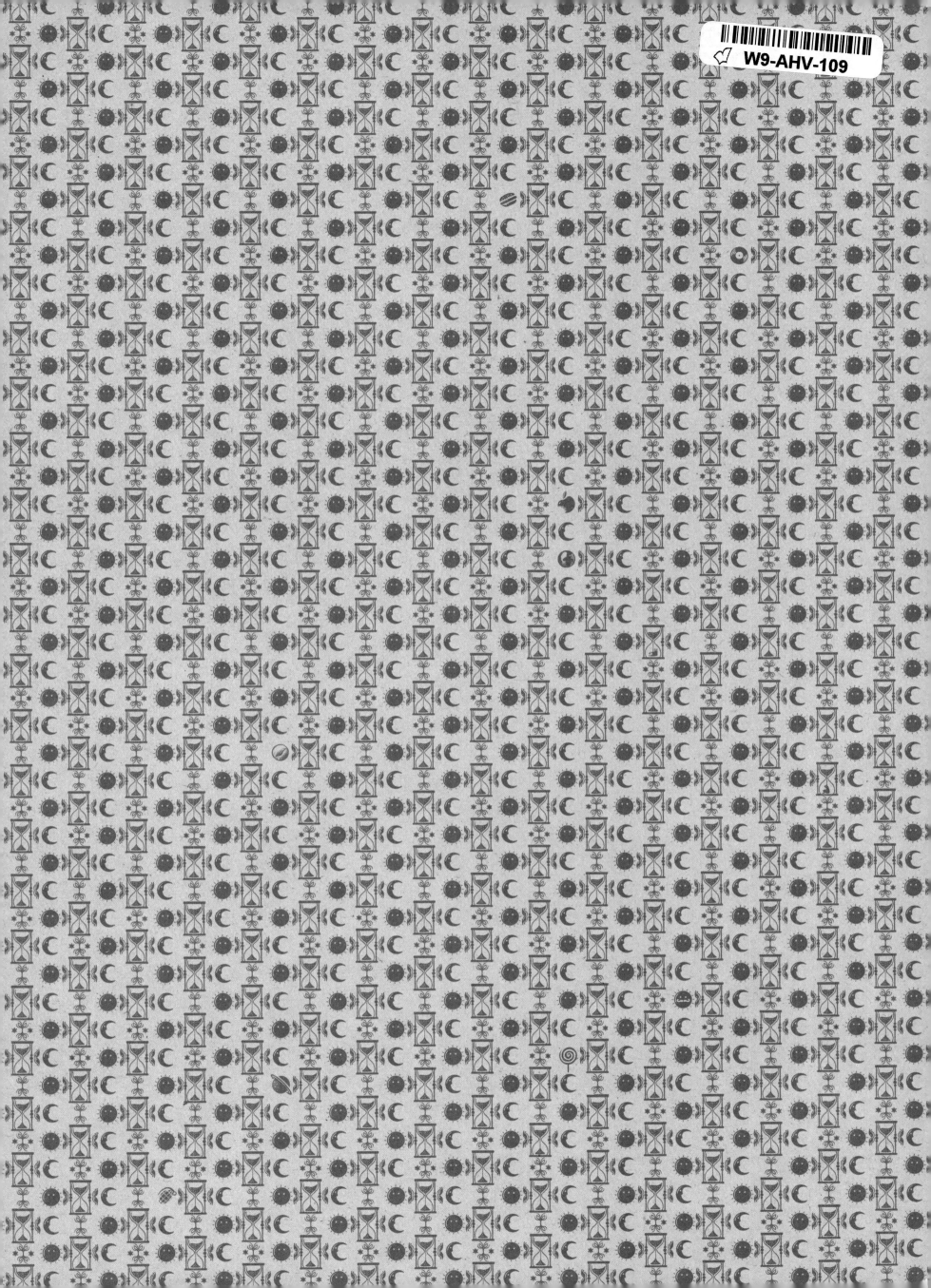

The BIG BANG!

Scientists believe that about 13.7 billion Earth years ago everything in the universe was compressed into a single red-hot point. During an enormous primordial explosion, time and matter were born from that tiny point.

Earth came into existence about 4.55 billion years ago.

TIMELINE

A Visual History of Our World

Peter Goes

GECKO PRESS

The beginning of life

It was some time before life appeared on Earth. Traces of life can still sometimes be found in prehistoric rocks. Such remains of plants or animals, called fossils, date back to various geological time periods. Every period has a name, and these are sometimes divided into shorter periods—for example, the Mesozoic Era is made up of three geological time periods: the Triassic, Jurassic, and Cretaceous.

Fish were the first creatures
vertebrae—the segments that form the backbone.
There were more than 15 000 species of trilobite.
Trilobites existed 521–250 million years ago, in the Paleozoic Era.
Stromatolites are Earth's oldest fossils—they could be up to 3.5 billion years old. Stromatolite fossils were formed by blue algae, a kind of primitive bacteria.
Trilobites are some of the oldest fossils on Earth.

Amphibians are thought to have existed from about 350 million years ago. They are animals, such as frogs and salamanders, which live partly on land and partly in water.
Ammonites lived 400–66 million years ago in the Paleozoic and Mesozoic eras.
There were hundreds of species of ammonite.
Ammonites are the extinct ancestors of the octopus.

The biggest flying creature of all time was Quetzalcoatl.

The word "dinosaur" is derived from the ancient Greek words "deinos" (terrible) and "sauros" (lizard).

The best-known dinosaur is the fearsome Tyrannosaurus rex. T. rex, Giganotosaurus, and Spinosaurus were the largest-ever land predators.

Insect fossils have been found that are up to 400 million years old.

The Titanosaurus was the giant among dinosaurs. A fossil of this plant eater was uncovered in Argentina in 2005. Its skeleton is 77 million years old.

The pterosaurs were not dinosaurs—they were flying reptiles.
They evolved more than 220 million years ago, in the Triassic Period.
Stegosaurus
Parasaurolophus
In the Mesozoic Era most plants were gymnosperms: ferns and conifers.
Triceratops
Baby triceratops

The dinosaurs

Dinosaurs lived about 230–65 million years ago, in the Mesozoic Era—from the late Triassic Period to the Cretaceous Period. No other vertebrates have lived over such a long period of time. There was a great diversity of dinosaurs, ranging from small bird-like species to the largest reptiles that ever walked the Earth. People used to think that dinosaur fossils belonged to dragons and monsters. It was not until the beginning of the 19th century that the first dinosaurs were identified.

The Chicxulub Crater is thought to be evidence of a meteorite collision that brought the age of the dinosaurs to an end.
Creatures that survived the disaster—which included many insects, amphibians, and mammals—continued evolving.

The end of the dinosaurs

The age of the dinosaurs came to a sudden end. The most likely explanation is that the impact of a massive meteorite at the end of the Cretaceous Period, about 65 million years ago, caused the dinosaurs' extinction. The crater the meteorite created is in Mexico and traces of it can still be seen today. It wasn't just the dinosaurs that perished; some three-quarters of all plant and animal species died out, making this one of the largest extinction events in Earth's history. But with the disappearance of the dinosaurs, mammals—including, eventually, humans—had their chance to evolve.

he impact of the meteorite caused huge dust and smoke clouds that blotted out the sun.
As a result, plants could no longer grow.

The oldest found fossils of owls are 65–56 million years old.
Mammoth
Another mammoth
During the last ice age people formed groups to hunt large mammals.
Woolly rhinoceros
Saber-toothed cat
In 1974, in the Afar region of Ethiopia, Donald C. Johanson discovered one of the oldest fossils of a human ancestor who walked on two legs. He named his find Lucy—the scientific name is Australopithecus afarensis. Lucy lived 3.5 million years ago.

About 45 000 years ago Homo sapiens arrived in Europe from Africa. Homo sapiens is Latin for "wise person."
15 000-year-old rock drawings were found in the cave of Altamira in Spain. The cave was discovered in 1879 and is now world famous.
Was the Venus of Willendorf a fertility symbol? This statuette of a woman, found by an archaeologist in 1908, is estimated to be 25 000 years old.
Neanderthals appeared around 200 000 years ago. Neanderthals lived in groups and used specialized tools, such as spears, chisels, and drills. They most likely died out when Homo sapiens arrived.

The first people

All prehistoric discoveries indicate that the first people came from Africa. These discoveries include tools made 3.3 million years ago by the ancestors of modern humans. Because the tools were fashioned from stone, this period is known as the Stone Age. Early humans hunted wild animals, and had to cope with the temperature swings of the ice ages—periods of intense cold—alternating with warmer periods. The last great ice age ended around 10 000 years ago. Over time, many different hominid (human-like) species evolved. None of them survive today except *Homo sapiens*—that's you and all the other people on Earth.

Megaliths—monuments made of giant stones—have been found all over the world. Little is known about the people who made them or what they were for.
Farming began in three locations at the same time: in the Fertile Crescent of the Middle East, in Central America, and in East Asia.
Dogs were among the first tamed animals. They descend from wolves.
Tools for farming and weapons for hunting were often made of flint, and also of antler, bone, and wood.

Village on stilts
The wheel
The oldest boat so far discovered was found in the Netherlands. The Pesse Canoe, made from a tree trunk, is dated between 8200 and 7600 BC.

The first settlements

For a long time people lived a nomadic existence, but eventually they stopped roving and settled in one place. Instead of hunting, people turned to farming. While these first farmers moved on as soon as the soil in a field was exhausted, they later discovered how to fertilize the soil, replenishing its nutrients so that fresh crops could grow. It was no longer necessary to move on. Today we call a large farm, a group of houses, or a small town a "settlement." The time of the first human settlements is called the Neolithic Era, or the New Stone Age. It began approximately 14 000 years ago.

Cuneiform script, an early writing system, was invented in Mesopotamia to keep track of goods and record agreements. Soon stories came to be written down, too. The Epic of Gilgamesh is a long narrative poem about the legendary king of Uruk. It is one of the oldest literary works in the world.
Sumerians and Akkadians founded various city-states more than 4000 years ago.
Lamassu is a demon from Persian mythology who helped people in the fight against evil.
A ziggurat is a temple tower.
The Tigris
Uruk was the most important Sumerian city.
The Mesopotamians counted in multiples of six. This system is still employed today, in timekeeping and working out angles.
The Amorite king Hammurabi brought an end to the fighting between city-states and became king of Babylon in 1792 BC. His kingdom was conquered centuries later by the Assyrians.

Mesopotamia

"Mesopotamia" is an ancient Greek word that means "between rivers." Several city-states—large cities that had their own government—sprang up along the fertile banks of the Tigris and Euphrates rivers, which flow through the region known today as the Middle East. The city-states merged into successive civilizations, including the Old Babylonian Empire, the Assyrian Empire, and the New Babylonian Empire. The rise of the Persian Empire brought an end to Babylonian rule. Today, Babylon is part of modern-day Iraq.

The Tower of Babel might have looked like this.
King Nebuchadnezzar II (634–562 BC) reigned over the New Babylonian Empire. He rebuilt the city of Babylon with streets and blocks of houses in a grid pattern, like a chessboard. His name is on nearly every brick of the ruins of his city wall.
The Babylonians believed that the movements of the stars and the planets were linked to the fate of the king and the empire. Babylonian stargazers are now recognized as the first astronomers.
Ashurbanipal (c.668–627 BC) was the last great ruler of Assyria. In the library of Nineveh, the first proper library in history, he collected thousands of clay tablets.
Cuneiform was developed sometime between 3300 and 2900 BC. Scribes wrote by pressing a reed into soft clay.
he Ishtar Gate is a remnant of the glorious Babylon of King Nebuchadnezzar II. Ishtar was the sky goddess.
The Hanging Gardens of Babylon were terraced rooftop gardens renowned in ancient times as one of the Seven Wonders of the World.
The Euphrates

King Menes is said to have united Upper and Lower Egypt into one kingdom, around 3000 BC.
The scarab, a dung beetle, was considered a sacred creature by the Egyptians. It was linked to Kheper, the god of the rising sun.
During the construction of a modern dam on the Nile—the Aswan—the old temples of Abu Simbel were threatened by flooding, so in 1964 they were taken apart and rebuilt on higher ground.
Most Egyptians were farmers.
The word "pharaoh" originally meant "big house" and referred to the palace of the royal couple who stood at the head of society. Much later "pharaoh" became the title for the actual king or queen.
Chickens were already scratching around in Egypt in 1400 BC.
Before the pyramids, the Egyptians buried their important dead in mastabas or tombs.

Ancient Egypt

The mighty Egyptian Empire developed around 3300 BC along the banks of the river Nile in northern Africa and lasted until 332 BC. The ancient Egyptian age is divided into three periods: the Old Kingdom, the Middle Kingdom, and the New Kingdom. The land, too, was at first divided: Lower Egypt lay by the delta (where the Nile empties into the Mediterranean Sea) and Upper Egypt lay to the south of the delta.

Of the ancient Seven Wonders of the World, only the pyramids of Giza remain. These tombs were built between 2551 and 2472 BC, during the Old Kingdom.
In 332 BC the Macedonian king Alexander the Great invaded and conquered Egypt, bringing an end to the 3000-year Egyptian Empire.
A sphinx is a mythological creature with the head of a person.
The sphinx at Giza was hewn from a giant rock formation.
Anubis, the god of the afterlife, weighs the souls of the dead.
arcophagus is a coffin made of stone.
ppopotamus
The Egyptians communicated and recorded information with hieroglyphics. These are not letters but a kind of pictogram.
Papyrus grows along the banks of the Nile. The Egyptians made the first paper from papyrus stalks.

Pegasus
There are three different types of Greek column.
Doric
Ionic
Corinthian
According to Greek mythology the gods lived on Olympus, the highest mountain in Greece.
The Panhellenic Games were the forerunners of the Olympic Games.
Marathon
The Trojan War plays a leading part in Greek stories, one of which is the tale of the wooden horse. In wartime, the Greeks captured the city of Troy using this clever deception.
In the 5th century BC, the Greek city-states defeated the Persians in two wars.
In about 1100 BC the Dorians invaded Greece from the northwest. They settled in Greece's largest peninsula, the Peloponnese, where they founded Sparta, capital city of their military state.

The Parthenon was the temple of the goddess Athena Parthenos. She was the protector goddess of the city of Athens.
Icarus
A hoplite was a foot soldier in the Greek army. Soldiers formed themselves into an easy-to-defend wall of shields and lances.
Actors moved from city to city, performing in the open air.
Democracy and the right to vote originated in the Archaic Period (c.800–480 BC). Slaves and women had no voting rights.
Eureka, eureka!
Archimedes (287–212 BC) was one of the greatest ever mathematicians.
Homer (c.800–750 BC) was a blind Greek poet. He wrote The Iliad and The Odyssey.
Socrates was an Athenian philosopher. He was sentenced to death for impiety in 399 BC and forced to drink a cup of poison.
The Hellenistic Period started in 323 BC with the conquests by Alexander the Great, who founded the Macedonian Empire. It ended when the Romans conquered Greece in 31 BC.

Ancient Greece

The legendary kingdom of King Minos flourished on the Greek island of Crete in the Neolithic Era, or the New Stone Age (around 4500 years ago). Later, in the Bronze Age, the Mycenaean civilization rose up in what is now Greece. Greek-speaking people established themselves along the Ionian coast, founding city-states. The best known of these are Athens and Sparta. A great rivalry existed between the two cities, and they were often at war. The classical Greek period—which we know from its temples, sculpture, and philosophy—lasted from the end of the Persian Wars (about 500 BC) to the death of Alexander the Great in 323 BC.

The earliest coat of mail ever found
came from the grave of a Celtic ruler
from the 4th century BC.
The Celts were known for the high quality of their metalwork.
The natural world was vitally important in the Celtic religion, and magic
powers were attributed to oak trees and the mistletoe that grew on the

Nearly all of the Celts' territory was conquered by the Roman legions. The Romans called the Celts of Western Europe "Gauls." Once defeated, the Celts became "Gallo-Roman," adopting the culture and language of their conquerors.
Ambiorix was one of the leaders of the Eburones, a Gallic tribe that resisted the Roman conquerors.
Hill fort
Sacred mistletoe
Druids played a leading role in Celtic culture. A druid was simultaneous priest, mediator, doctor, scientist, and judge.
The carnyx was a copper wind instrument.
The warlike Celts often fought naked.
In the Celtic mythology of Ireland, Dagda is father of the gods.
Crannogs were artificial islands in Scotland.
Vercingetorix was the king who led the Gallic uprising against the Romans in 53–52 BC.

The Celts

The Celts inhabited a great deal of Europe from 650 BC onward. They originated from a variety of tribes with a common language and culture. Other languages derived from the old Celtic: Irish, Scots, Breton, and Welsh. The names of many European streams and rivers—such as Danube, Meuse, Thames, Trent—betray their Celtic roots. The Celts were regularly at loggerheads with the Roman occupiers, but there were also Celts who worked with the Romans.

According to legend, Rome was founded in 753 BC by the twins Romulus and Remus, who were raised by a wolf.

SPQR

The Romans fought three wars against the inhabitants of Carthage, an African trading town, known as the Punic Wars. The first was settled at sea. During the second war the Carthaginian general Hannibal crossed the Alps with elephants to reach Rome. In the final war (in 146 BC), Carthage was razed.

The first emperor of Rome was Augustus (63 BC–14 AD), the adopted son of Julius Caesar. The word "kaiser" is derived from the name Caesar.

VENI VIDI VICI

The emperor Nero (37–68 AD), notorious for his cruelty, had a gigantic statue made of himself.

Aqueduct

Julius Caesar (100–44 BC) was a successful statesman and general.

Gladiators fought in the Colosseum to entertain the population of Rome.

The senate was the most influential political body during the Roman republic.

Military roads were broad, paved, and straight. They formed a widespread network throughout Europe.

According to the Bible, Jesus Christ was born during the reign of the emperor Augustus. In 381 AD Christianity became the official religion of the Roman Empire.

The Roman Empire

Rome initially consisted of a few settlements of Latins in what is now Italy. In the 7th century BC the Etruscans occupied these settlements and combined them into a town, ruled for 150 years by Etruscan kings. The Latins largely adopted their writing, religion, and culture. In 509 BC the last Etruscan king was deposed and Rome was declared a republic, with elected leaders. This powerful republic came to an end in the 1st century BC when civil war broke out and Augustus declared himself emperor. Augustus's reign was a time of relative peace and a golden age of literature from writers such as Virgil, Ovid, Horace, and Livy. The Roman Empire flourished for centuries but eventually began to lose power. Late in the 5th century AD Germanic tribes crossed the borders, and the Western Roman Empire was overthrown.

The Picts and the Celts
The emperor Hadrian built a wall to protect the Romans' conquered lands in Great Britain.
The Romans called the Mediterranean Sea Mare Nostrum, Latin for "our sea."
ROMA
ROMA
Triumphal arch
Legionaries were professional soldiers. Their service lasted many years.
The testudo, or tortoise, formation
The borders of the empire were guarded by strategically placed forts.
Rome was plundered several times during its history. In 410 AD Alaric, the king of the Visigoths, was the first German to occupy Rome.
Milestone

The Huns

In the 4th century AD the Huns, a collection of nomadic people from the Asian steppes, entered Europe. Their raids drove the Germanic people westward into the weakened Roman Empire. Attila, who was the khan of the Huns from 434 until his sudden death in 453, was given the nickname "scourge of God." He succeeded in uniting the various tribes, but his kingdom fell apart shortly after his death.

In 451 a decisive pitched battle between the Huns and the Romans took place in the northeast of what is now France. This brought an end to the Huns' raids in Western Europe.

The Huns fought with composite bows made of wood, horn, and sinew, which they used on horseback. Once stretched, the bowstring would remain taut—a very useful feature.

The Huns were closely related to the Scythians, who arrived before them, as well as to the Magyars, Turks, and Mongolians, who later followed them. All of these peoples were deadly, high-speed raiders on horseback.

Attila the Hun was the most feared enemy of the whole Roman Empire.
Attila died of intoxication and a violent nosebleed during his seventh wedding.
According to legend an old man brought Attila a sword that had fallen from the sky. The Romans named it "the sword of Mars" after the Roman god of war.
A yurt is a quickly assembled and easily transported nomad's tent made of felt, poles, and straps.

The influence of the Byzantine Empire extended internationally due to its well-developed diplomacy.
Crusaders of the fourth crusade seized Constantinople in 1204 and established a Latin government. When this government fell in 1261, the citizens of Byzantium returned to their city.
Constantinople lay on the Silk Road, a network of trade routes linking the Far East and the West. Silk was a very expensive commodity from China.
During sea battles the Byzantines used their dreaded weapon "Greek fire" to set enemy ships ablaze.

Byzantium was founded by Greeks in 667 BC. In the Byzantine Empire it was called Constantinople, and today it is Istanbul, in Turkey.
Justinian I came to the throne in 527. He recaptured a great deal of the Western Roman Empire from the Germans. The splendid Hagia Sophia is one of the hundreds of churches he built.
Faith played a large part in daily life.
Hagia Sophia
During the height of the Byzantine Empire, Basil I (867–886) conquered territory reaching to the Euphrates in the east and to south Italy in the west.

The Byzantine Empire

The Roman Empire was divided into east and west from the 3rd century AD. In 330 the emperor Constantine moved his capital from Rome to Byzantium in the east. It was renamed Nova Roma or "New Rome" but soon became known as Constantinople. When the Roman Empire in the west fell in 476, the Eastern Roman Empire was renamed the Byzantine Empire. The people called themselves Roman, although they spoke Greek rather than Latin and their art and culture were Greek-inspired. Even their Christian belief had its own slant, and the Greek church split from the Roman church in 1054. Later in the century the Islamic Seljuks threatened the borders of the empire, and despite the earlier split from the Roman church, the Byzantine emperor asked the pope for military support. This resulted in the first of nine crusades by Christians of the west who wanted to free the Holy Land and Jerusalem. Eventually the Ottomans (successors of the Seljuks) captured Constantinople in 1453, bringing the Byzantine Empire to an end.

The Middle Ages

After the fall of the Roman Empire in the west in 476, the next thousand years in Europe were called the Middle Ages, or medieval period. Harried by the Huns, Germanic tribes such as the Franks re-established themselves throughout Europe. Around 800 the Middle Ages experienced its first high point, a period known as the Carolingian Renaissance. Charlemagne was the greatest ruler of the Carolingian Empire and the Franks. He united most of Western Europe. Three hundred years later the cities gained power and strength, and trade was strong with the whole known world. Christian belief was the foundation of society.

Clovis I was the leader of the Salian Franks. He converted to Christianity and became an ally of the church. He was baptized in Reims in 496.
Society was feudal. A liege lord—the king, for example—loaned parts of his land to a vassal, or tenant. In return the vassal promised military help and some produce from the land.
Paris was the capital city of the Merovingian Empire.

By the 11th century knightly romances had been written about the life of Charlemagne, including Le Chanson de Roland (The Song of Roland), about his defeat in the pass of Roncesvalles.

Mohammed, the prophet who would found Islam, was born in Mecca (c.570).

In 800 the pope crowned Charlemagne the first ruler of the Holy Roman Empire.

Monks withdrew to abbeys to devote themselves to study and prayer.

Before the rise of the towns in the 12th century, society in the Middle Ages could be divided roughly into three groups: those who prayed (the clergy), those who fought (the nobility), and those who worked (the farmers).

Charlemagne's white war elephant, Abul-Abbas, was a gift from the caliph of Baghdad.

Troubadours were roaming musicians and poets. A minstrel was a musician with a permanent place in a noble household.

Most of the population was not free: people were bound to their lords and their land, many little better off than slaves.

In the 9th century the Vikings founded Dublin, in Ireland. Alfred the Great, king of Wessex, made a stand and offered the Vikings a part of England—known as the Danelaw.
Thor, the god of thunder
Ratatosk climbed the "world tree" to bring news of the dragon at the foot of the tree to the eagle at the top.
Beowulf was a Danish hero who took on the monster Grendel.
Rollo, the leader of the Vikings, and his Norsemen settled in the north of France. Their descendants, the Normans, would conquer England under the leadership of William the Conqueror in 1066.
The karve and the knarr were types of Viking ship.
The Vikings were the best shipbuilders of their time.
Churches were built in Romanesque style. The Vikings knew they could find treasure inside these holy buildings. Later, the Vikings converted to Christianity.
Runes are the letters that formed the oldest alphabet of the Germanic peoples.

The Vikings

Between 789 and 1100, seafaring warriors from Scandinavia scoured the European coasts in search of plunder. At first the Vikings targeted monasteries because they contained many valuables and the monks were unarmed. Later they attacked towns at river mouths. But the Vikings were not just plunderers. At home they were farmers, and during their sea voyages they traded goods. They discovered and settled Iceland and Greenland, and gained footholds in Ireland, Scotland, England, and France. They may have reached America before Christopher Columbus. With fertile ground scarce at home, the Vikings were always in search of new lands to farm.

The Crusades

When Byzantium lost more territory to the Muslims, Emperor Alexius I Comnenus asked Pope Urban II for help. In 1095 the pope responded and called for an armed pilgrimage. Swept up by hearsay about the torture, persecution, and massacre of pilgrims, Christians in the West felt they had to answer the pope's call, and whole families took part in the crusade to free Jerusalem. After a journey on foot that lasted four awful years, the Christians raised their tents at Jerusalem. On July 15, 1099, the city fell, but the occupation degenerated into a bloodbath. Following the defeat of Jerusalem, four Christian cities were founded in the Middle East. To defend them, a number of crusades followed. The last true crusade took place from 1271 to 1272. In 1291 the final Christian stronghold fell into Muslim hands. This marked the end of the crusading period.

Richard I of England, otherwise known as Richard the Lionheart, took part in the third crusade. While he never reached Jerusalem, he did defeat Saladin, the sultan who succeeded in uniting the Muslims. Saladin and Richard later made a treaty.
Jerusalem is a holy place for the three monotheistic religions: Judaism, Christianity, and Islam.
The Templars were fighting monks whose role was to protect pilgrims. They were called Templars because their headquarters were on the Temple Mount in Jerusalem.

Robert the Bruce, the king of Scotland, defeated the English army in 1314, preserving Scotland's independence.

Flemish wool weavers settled in Leeds in England, giving the city increased trade status.

Margaret I was queen of Denmark, Norway, and Sweden.

In 1302 the townspeople of Bruges murdered members of the French garrison and pro-French citizens. They called this "Good Friday," but it was later renamed the "Bruges Matins" after matins, the first prayers of the day.

The Renaissance (meaning "rebirth") began in Italy, celebrating the ancient culture of the Greeks and Romans.

The great famine of 1315 to 1317 claimed millions of lives.

A bombard or early cannon

From 1309 until 1377 the popes did not live in Rome, but in Avignon, France. Although the popes chose to stay there, they were still at the mercy of the French king.

Władysław the Short united Poland in

In retaliation for the Bruges Matins the French king sent his army to Flanders. The Flemish forces decimated the French army at the Battle of Courtrai, also known as the Battle of the Golden Spurs.

4th century is considered the high of Gothic architecture and art.
When clock towers became common, people started to divide the days into hours.
From 1370 Timur Lenk, or Tamerlane, ruled Central Asia, where he founded the Timurid Empire.
People who performed the same job or craft created professional associations called guilds.
In 1381 English farmers rose up against their oppressive lords. The Peasants' Revolt failed but set in motion the abolition of serfdom.
The plague, or Black Death, raged from 1347 to 1351. It killed an estimated one-third of the population of Europe, at that time several tens of millions.
The English writer Geoffrey Chaucer composed The Canterbury Tales in Middle English. In the tales, a group of pilgrims tell stories on their way to Canterbury.
In 1358 French peasants rose up against the nobility. The revolt was known as the Jacquerie, after the name Jacques Bonhomme (Jack Goodfellow), which nobles used arrogantly to refer to any peasant.
The Italian poet Dante wrote The Divine Comedy, a long poem in three parts describing his imaginary journey to hell, purgatory, and paradise.

The 14th century

At the beginning of the 14th century it suddenly became colder, and it rained a great deal. The worsening weather caused poor harvests and severe famine. In the wake of the famine, the plague (a disease dating back to Roman times) reappeared. The plague bacteria spread very quickly via the same trade routes that had brought so much prosperity. The already-starving population died in great numbers. To make matters worse, a war between France and England raged for one hundred years. But the 14th century also produced better things: learning and art began to flourish in Italy, for example.

Suleyman I and his wife Roxelana stee[r]ed the Ottoman Empire to a golden age in the 16th century. They made Istanbul the heart of the Islamic world.
Sultan Mehmed II conquered Constantinople in 1453. The fall of the city and the death in battle of Constantine XI marked the end of both the Byzantine Empire and the Middle Ages.
Osman I, founder of the Ottoman dynasty in Anatolia

In 1571 the allied Christian forces defeated the Islamic fleet of the Ottoman Empire at Lepanto in Greece—the last battle fought with galleys. Among the Christian fighters was Miguel de Cervantes, who later wrote Don Quixote.
The Galata Tower in Istanbul survives from the Byzantine era.
One of the largest observatories of the Islamic world was built in Istanbul in 1577. Here the astronomer Taqi ad-Din studied the heavens.
Oil wrestling
The tanbur was a lute-like stringed instrument.
Muhammad Ali founded modern Egypt early in the 19th century.
Mustafa Ataturk was an Ottoman army officer who became the first president of the Turkish Republic in 1923.
The borders of Turkey were fixed in 1923, following the Greco–Turkish war of 1921–1922.
In 1915, during World War I, Australian and New Zealand soldiers clashed with soldiers of the Ottoman Empire at Gallipoli. After a hard-fought battle, the Turks triumphed.

The Ottoman Empire

Towards the end of the 13th century the Byzantine Empire had lost most of its power in Asia Minor (an old name for Turkey and adjacent regions). In its place, Osman I, leader of the Turks, established the Ottoman Empire. The Ottomans gave up their nomadic way of life, and their empire grew to become a world power between the 14th and the 20th centuries; at one time it covered an enormous territory in North Africa, Europe, and Asia. The Ottoman Empire reached its high point in the 16th century. At that time the Ottomans held sway over the Black Sea, the Red Sea, and a great deal of the Mediterranean. The end came in 1922, following defeat in World War I.

Confucius was a Chinese philosopher who lived long before the Ming Dynasty (551–479 BC). His teaching was called Confucianism—a way of life and ideology that has remained significant for centuries.
The Great Wall of China was constructed largely during the Ming Dynasty to protect China against enemy raiders from the steppes.
Rice paddies
The first Ming emperor, a rebel leader with peasant origins, wanted a kingdom of farming villages and compulsory military service.
Kung fu is a Chinese martial art.
Cormorants, fish-eating aquatic birds, were trained to catch fish at night.

The Ming Dynasty

China has one of the oldest cultures in the world, with origins five to seven thousand years ago. Centuries ago the country was ruled by dynasties. A dynasty began with an emperor, whom people believed had a divine right to rule, and continued with that emperor's descendants. In adversity, or if the people were unhappy, the old emperor had to give way to another and to a new dynasty. The Ming Dynasty ruled China from 1368 until 1644: during these three centuries of stable rule people made great discoveries and trade flourished.

The emperors of the Ming Dynasty, and of the Qing Dynasty that followed it, ruled the kingdom from the Forbidden City in Peking (Beijing).
Chinese people followed Confucius but could also practice Buddhism. Buddhist monks lived in monasteries.
Wan Hu is said to have used fireworks to make a rocket to send himself to the moon.
Chinese vases from the Ming Dynasty are world renowned.
Nanjing was the biggest port in the world.
Admiral Zheng He made seven voyages of discovery between 1405 and 1433.
Japan invaded Korea twice between 1592 and 1598, with the intent to conquer China.

The 15th century

The invention of printing had a huge impact worldwide. Books could quickly spread new ideas. In the 15th century, the Hundred Years' War between France and England came to an end as well. The long and costly war had, however, helped the cloth trade to flourish in what is now Belgium and the Netherlands. In the east, Byzantium had been defeated by the Ottomans. It was a new dawn.

The final battle in the Hundred Years' War between France and England took place in 1453 at Castillon, in the south of France.
Joan of Arc
As a sixteen-year-old farm girl, Joan of Arc led the French to victory over the English during the Hundred Years' War. Three years later, in 1431, she fell into the hands of the English, who condemned her for witchcraft and burned her at the stake. Now Joan of Arc is the patron saint of France.

The Wars of the Roses (1455–1485) between the noble English families of Lancaster and York received their name because Lancaster bore a red rose on its coat of arms and York a white. Both "houses" fought for the royal title.

Leonardo da Vinci (1452–1519) was a multitalented genius from Florence, Italy. Creator of the famous Mona Lisa, he was not only an artist but also an inventor, architect, philosopher, physicist, writer, and composer.

Ghent and Bruges had become very rich and powerful cities.

..., son of Vlad II Dracul, was a prince of Wallachia, ...omania, in the middle of the century. His nickname, Vlad the Impaler, refers to his cruelty.

The Spanish Inquisition was established by the Spanish king in 1478 to investigate converts from Judaism and, later, heretics.

...onstantinople fell in 1453, signifying ...the end of the Byzantine Empire.

The Lamb of God is a masterpiece by Flemish Primitive painters Jan and Hubert van Eyck.

The German Johannes Gutenberg (c. 1398–1468) became known as the inventor of the printing process. In fact, the technique was already in use in 11th-century China.

Machu Picchu was never discovered by the Spanish so was known as the "hidden city." It is 2400 m (7874 ft) above sea level.
The condor is a bird of prey found in the Andean mountain range.
The Inca sun god Inti
Pumpkins and tomatoes
The Incas had an extensive network of paved walkways and suspension bridges.
Inca temple
The Amazon rainforest
Pineapple
Many types of fruits, vegetables, and grains—including maize and potatoes—were first cultivated in Central and South America. Later they were exported to Europe.
Spanish conquerors in the 16th century were on the hunt for

The Incas

As the Middle Ages were coming to an end in Europe, on the other side of the world major cultures were beginning to flourish. One of these was the Incas. In the 13th century the Incas were just a tribe in the highlands of Peru, but in the 15th century they spread quickly across the west coast of South America. They were no match, however, for the invaders from Europe. After Christopher Columbus reached the Americas in 1492, the Spanish sent waves of conquistadors—conquerors—to spread the Catholic faith and build foreign trade. The Incas' mighty empire then collapsed under the weight of disease and violence brought by the conquistadors.

The Aztecs

The Aztecs, a nation of warriors, settled in Central America in the early 13th century and founded a powerful empire. Their greatest city was Tenochtitlan, which lay in the middle of a marshy lake. The Spanish conquistador Hernán Cortés conquered the Aztec Empire between 1519 and 1521. The Aztec emperor Montezuma had believed that the arrival of the Spanish fulfilled an ancient prophecy so he offered them hospitality. But things ended badly for the Aztecs. Not only did fighting break out, but the Spanish also brought with them diseases against which the Aztecs had no resistance. Many died, including Montezuma.

When Aztec priests saw an eagle battling a snake on a cactus, they told their people to settle at that place. In 1325, on an island in Lake Texcoco, the city of Tenochtitlan was established—the present-day Mexico City.
The Aztecs carried out human sacrifice on a large scale, which is why they kept prisoners of war. This made them unpopular with nearby peoples, who united with the Spanish against them.
Cacao trees
Maize fields
The water goddess Chalchiuhtlicue
The Aztecs called themselves the Mexica.
Potatoes
Aztec warriors
Spanish missionaries
The island of San Salvador was Christopher Columbus's first port of call.
Niña
Santa María
Pinta

On a voyage funded by the king and queen of Spain, the Italian explorer Christopher Columbus sailed west in search of a sea route to Asia, but instead he reached the "New World".

Nicolaus Copernicus put forward the theory that the solar system revolved around the sun, not Earth—challenging the earlier theory of Greek mathematican and astronomer Ptolemy.
The Eighty Years War, which raged between 1568 and 1648, led to the separation of the northern Netherlands from the control of Spain.
Ivan IV, tsar of Russia from 1547 until h death in 1584, was tyrannical and violent and so was known as Ivan the Terrible.
It was said that the empire of Charles V was one on which the sun never set.
Johann Faust was a German doctor, astrologer, and magician. People claimed that he had made a pact with the devil.
The English king Henry VIII reigned from 1509 to 1547. He broke away from the Church of Rome because the pope would not let him divorce. He married six times.
Some people believe that the apothecary, astrologer, and fortune-teller Nostradamus (1503–1566) has predicted all important world events.
Michelangelo painted the frescos in the Sistine Chapel between 1508 and 1512. He was also an architect, sculptor, and poet.
Zeal for reform created a backlash against Catholic art. Churches and religious all over Europe were attacked and religious statues and artworks dest

Italian Galileo Galilei disagreed with Ptolemy. He came
to conflict with the church and, already an old man,
was put under lifelong house arrest in 1633.
The Renaissance gave fresh impetus to painting, sculpture, architecture, philosophy, and science. Italy was at the heart of this regeneration.
The Mongolians, skilled horseback raiders, invaded China and besieged Peking (Beijing) in 1550.
The Spanish Fury refers to the sacking of Antwerp in 1576. Rebel soldiers from the Spanish army set fire to the city and created a bloodbath.
England flourished during the reign of Queen Elizabeth I, daughter of King Henry VIII, during the second half of the 16th century.
In 1517 monk and theologian Martin Luther wrote a letter to the pope criticizing the Catholic Church. This was the start of Protestantism, or the Reformation.
William Shakespeare, an English actor, poet, and playwright
es van Wesele, or Andreas Vesalius,
ne of the founders of anatomical studies.
Spain and England were at war from 1585 until 1604. Each commanded a large navy.

The 16th century

In Europe, people began to criticize the Catholic Church. Martin Luther, a German monk, preached a new, "reformed" Christendom, which would go on to become the Protestant Reformation. With the increased availability of printing presses, Luther's ideas and those of other reformers spread quickly. Uprisings broke out, but Charles V, who as Holy Roman Emperor held sway over much of Europe, suppressed the revolts with a heavy hand. He wanted obedience to the Catholic Church within his borders: one kingdom, one ruler, one faith. Lesser nobles saw an opportunity, and they supported Luther when he was expelled from the church. They did not want any more interference from church and emperor in their principalities. Science and art were both very important in the 16th century. People looked with wonder at ancient culture, as if it were something new, which was why some called the 16th century the Renaissance (the "rebirth").

The American Robert Peary reached the North Pole in 1909, but his rival, Frederick Cook, was there as well. Both claimed to have been there first.

The Danes made sco[...] expeditions to Green[...] from 1605 to [...]

The Russians reached Alaska in the 17th century.

Erik the Red explored the coast of Greenland c. 982.

Leif Erikson may have reached North America c. 1000.

Daniel Boone explored Kentucky in 1775.

The Venetian Giovanni Caboto, known as John Cabot, became an explorer in the service of England. He rediscovered North America in 1497.

Christopher Columbus reached America in 1492.

Between 1831 and 1836 Charles Darwin sailed the world on the HMS Beagle. He was a naturalist who laid the foundations for the theory of evolution.

America was named after Amerigo Vespucci, who, in 1499, explored parts of its interior.

In 1520 Portuguese explorers in search of legendary Christian ki[...] of Prester John arr[...] in Ethiopia.

The first European to enter the Amazon basin was the Spanish conquistador Francisco de Orellana in 1546.

The Dutch explorer Jacob Roggeveen accidentally came upon Easter Island in 1722.

With his ship the HMS Endeavour, British navigator and explorer James Cook led three expeditions through the Pacific Ocean, reaching New Zealand and Australia.

Here be dragons.

Explorers from all periods

People have always wanted to see what lies beyond the horizon. People of the Middle Ages dreamed of distant lands and fantasized about beings who were like us, but also very different. At the end of the 16th century European rulers competed to extend their territories overseas. They paid seafarers to find new lands and shorter trading routes. Missionaries voyaged far and wide to convert non-Christian peoples—they were explorers too.

N
Yakov Permyakov was a merchant and a Cossack. In 1712 he discovered the Lyakhovsky Islands in the East Siberian Sea.
The Italian friar Odoric of Pordenone was one of the greatest explorers of the late Middle Ages. His travels took him through a large part of Asia.
e Flemish cartographer Gerard de Kremer
an innovative, more reliable map of the world.
A Flemish Franciscan friar, Willem van Rubroeck, was sent by the French king as ambassador to Mongolia between 1253 and 1255.
The Dane Vitus Bering undertook the Kamchatka Expeditions (1725–1741) in the service of Russia. He explored Alaska as well as the strait that bears his name.
Zhang Qian was an ambassador of the Chinese emperor from the 2nd century BC who expanded the Silk Road.
In the Middle Ages the Venetian merchant and explorer Marco Polo crossed Asia with a caravan (a group of pilgrims or traders).
Between 1405 and 1433, during the Ming Dynasty, Zheng He undertook seven voyages with a fleet of junks.
Morton crossed nd explored Congo River 1874 to 1877.
Ferdinand Magellan was the first to almost circumnavigate the Earth. After his death in 1521, in the Philippines, his crew completed the voyage.
The Portuguese searched for a sea route to India for their trade in spices, and it was Vasco de Gama who found one. In 1498 he was the first to reach the coast of India via Africa.
Early Polynesian people were skilled navigators whose migration through East Polynesia began after 1 AD.
The Dutch galleon The Lion explored the southwest coast of Australia in 1622. Australia was then named New Holland.
he first European to sail past the most outherly point of Africa, the Cape of Good Hope, was the Portuguese Bartolomeu Dias, in 1488.
Dutch navigator Abel Tasman reached New Zealand, Australia, and Tonga during his voyage of 1642–1644.
In 1911 the Norwegian Roald Amundsen was the first to reach the South Pole.
The Discovery Expedition explored Antarctica from 1901 to 1904.

The French, English, and Dutch colonized North America. The Dutch founded New Amsterdam, later called New York.
In 1620 the Mayflower, a ship carrying English Puritan immigrants, docked in America. In England, the Pilgrims had felt restricted because of their religious beliefs.
In 1692 mass hysteria spread in the Purita town of Salem and roughly 20 "witches were hanged.
Isaac Newton, famous for the story of the falling apple, described the law of gravity in 1687.
The great fire of London in 166
In 1605 Cervantes wrote Don Quixote, one of the first novels in a modern European language (Spanish).
The French philosopher René Descartes rejected the centuries-old philosophy of Aristotle and designed his own system of thought. His "I think, therefore I am" model established the base for rationalism.
The British doctor William Harvey described blood circulation in 1628.
The Thirty Years' War (1618–1648) broke out between the reformed and Catholic countries in Europe.
Flemish diplomat and baroque painter Peter Paul Rubens
Tulips were imported to Europe from the Ottoman Empire in the 16th century. In the Netherlands this exotic flower enjoyed enormous popularity: in January 1637 a tulip bulb was worth as much as a house.
The tsars of the House of R ruled Russia from 1613 until t revolution in 1917.

The 17th century

During the 17th century the nations of Europe competed for international wealth and influence. After its break from Spanish control in 1585, the Dutch Republic became a world power, and with its fleet of 2000 ships it controlled the seas. But England was also a seafaring nation, and conflicts arose between the two countries. The Counter-Reformation of the previous century restored the influence of the Catholic Church in some countries. Art in the highly ornate baroque style was chiefly used to glorify the faith. Scientific enterprise was also prevalent. In France, kings further increased their power, and it was a time of absolute monarchy. But in England the king, Charles I, was beheaded, and a new form of government was established. Migration to America increased, now that several European nations had colonies or trading posts there.

The baroque style of architecture was a reminder of classical antiquity.
Louis XIV of France (1638–1715) is reputed to have said, "L'état c'est moi"—"I am the state." The story is not true, but the Sun King certainly believed he was above the law.
Musketeers carried swords along with their muskets, because the muskets were difficult to reload.
A civil war between 1639 and 1651 ended with the beheading of King Charles I and the replacement of the monarchy with the English Commonwealth.
Dutch scientist Antonie van Leeuwenhoek made a microscope much more powerful than those of his rivals.
The plays of Molière poked fun at the church but were beloved by French high society.
Dutch painter Rembrandt van Rijn
The English and the Dutch waged war at sea to gain control of the trade routes.
The flightless dodo lived on the island of Mauritius, where Dutch sailors anchored to restock their provisions. They killed so many dodos for food that the birds became extinct in 1693.

English author Daniel Defoe wrote the adventure novel Robinson Crusoe in 1719.

The notorious pirate Blackbeard captured at least 20 ships.

In 1707 the kingdoms of Scotland and England were joined as the United Kingdom, or the Kingdom of Great Britain.

England and Spain were at war again from 1727 until 1729.

German composer Johann Sebastian Bach

From 1757 until 1858 the British East India Company was in charge of the whole Indian subcontinent. The territory was then ruled by Britain until 1947.

Antonio Stradivari is the most famous violin maker of all time.

Holy Roman Empress Maria Theresa ruled over large empire and was regarded as one of the most influential and enlightened absolute monarchs.

The War of the Spanish Succession (1701–1713)

The piano was developed from the harpsichord early in the 18th century.

The baroque period was followed by the rococo, an artistic style characterized by fanciful shell and flower motifs.

Wolfgang Amadeus Mozart and his sister Anna Maria were musical prodigies who performed around Europe. A brilliant composer, Mozart was only 35 when he died in 1791.

In 1796 the English drove the Dutch out of Ceylon, the present-day Sri Lanka.

Two brothers, sons of the wealthy paper manufacturer Montgolfier, invented the hot-air balloon after seeing a shirt billowing in the warm air of an open fire. The first balloon flight with passengers took place in 1783.
Frederick the Great, king of Prussia
War of the Polish Succession (1733–1738)
Catherine the Great was tsarina of Russia from 1762 until 1796. She was said to have had many suitors.
Mont Blanc was called Mont Maudit, or "cursed mountain," until the Enlightenment, when people stopped believing in curses. The mountain's peak was first scaled in 1786.
The philosopher and writer Voltaire was the most important representative of the Enlightenment. His ideas underpinned the French Revolution.
The most famous work by Italian composer and violinist Antonio Vivaldi is The Four Seasons.
English poet and illustrator William Blake
In 1799 the Corsican general Napoleon Bonaparte took command of France. Five years later he crowned himself emperor.
y 14 is the National Day of France. It commemorates the 1789 storming of the Bastille—
dieval fortress and prison in Paris—which marked the beginning of the French Revolution.
Only seven people were imprisoned in the Bastille at the time, but a lot of ammunition was stored there.
Napoleon's troops invaded Egypt, where the French soldiers found a stone inscribed with three languages: the Rosetta Stone. Egyptian hieroglyphs could finally be deciphered.

The 18th century in Europe

The arts flourished in the 18th century. Mozart, Bach, and Vivaldi were renowned composers. Philosophy continued to build on the rationalism of the 17th century. This new intellectual movement, based on reason, was called the Enlightenment and was especially influential in France. Empiricism dominated in Great Britain: knowledge was obtained through experience, not just reason. In England new methods of farming were discovered, raising production dramatically. The British Empire grew in power, expanding as far as India. France, too, would build an empire, but not before a violent revolution.

The American printer, politician, and scientist Benjamin Franklin invented the lightning rod in 1752 and experimented with electricity.
Spanish Franciscans built more than 20 mission posts between 1769 and 1823 in the Spanish colony of California.
Enslaved Africans worked on plantations in the colonies.
Slave ships were filled to capacity to push down the "per item" cost. Much profit was made from this traffic in human beings.
In the French and Indian War (1754–1763) the French colonists fought side by side with Native Americans against the numerically superior British colonists.

The Founding Fathers is the name given to the organizers of the United States of America. In 1776 they signed the Declaration of Independence.
The first president of the United States was George Washington. He governed from 1789 until 1797.
We the People
The New York Stock Exchange has existed since 1792.
In 1789 the Constitution of the United States became law. Many other countries later took this constitution as their model.
John Adams helped write the Declaration of Independence. He succeeded George Washington as president in 1797.
The British colonies in America wanted to be independent of Great Britain. This led to the War of Independence or Revolutionary War (1775–1783).
The White House is the official residence of the American president.
In 1773 American colonists threw a shipment of tea into Boston Harbor in protest against a new British law regarding its import. This incident became known as the Boston Tea Party.

North America in the 18th century

As more and more Europeans settled in North America, the Native Americans were pushed off their ancestral lands. Many died from introduced diseases, to which they had no immunity, or in fighting with the newcomers. The European colonists used people brought from Africa as slaves to work their crops and in their homes, particularly in the south. The colonists, calling themselves "Americans," rose up in revolution against the British to create a new independent nation: the United States.

Otto Lilienthal was a German designer of gliders.
The kingdoms of Great Britain and Ireland united in 1801. The Irish opposed this union, sometimes violently, for the next hundred years.
The Romantic movement in the arts emphasized emotion and drama.
Greece became independent of the Ottoman Empire in 1832.
Belgium and the Netherlands joined in 1815 bu separated again in 1830. The German prince Leop became the first king of Belgium a year later.
Napoleon Bonaparte was emperor of France. Early in the 19th century he conquered a great deal of Europe. In 1815 he was defeated at Waterloo, and exiled to the island of Saint Helena.
Railway tracks were laid through all of Europe.
The first commercial train service began in England in 1825.
The invention of tin cans in 1810 improved food preservation.
From 1815 until the Austro–Prussian War of 1866, a number of independent states formed the German Confederation.
In 1903 the Women's Social and Political Union was established in England. The suffragettes strived for women's rights and votes for women.
VOTES FOR WOMEN
Thomas Edison, the American credited inventing the electric light bulb, establis the firm General Electric in 1889.
René Laënnec of France invented the stethoscope in 1816.
Italy was unified between 1859 and 1870.
Ludwig van Beethoven was a German composer whose works still influence modern music. He continued to compose even after he lost most of his hearing in the years before his death in 1827.
The Belgian Jozef De Veuster, or Father Damien, cared for lepers banished to the island of Molokai, Hawaii. He too contracted leprosy and died in 1889.

The 19th century

It could be said that the 19th century lasted until 1914: when World War I broke out, everything changed. Napoleon I was defeated in 1815, and the old empires collapsed amidst fresh revolutions and revolts. Modern countries started taking shape, and in imitation of American independence, other colonies began to free themselves from Europe. Driven by poverty or a desire for adventure, many people left Europe to begin new lives elsewhere. Industrialization began after the invention of the steam engine: factories sprang up everywhere. Cities became dirty and overcrowded. In their search for raw materials to support the new industries, European nations tried to annex new colonial territories, particularly in Africa.

The first motorized plane was invented in 1903 by the Wright brothers.

German philosopher Friedrich Nietzsche challenged the foundations of Christianity and traditional morality.

Karl Marx (1818–1883) gave his name to the ideology Marxism.

Otto von Bismarck, prime minister of Prussia (1862–1890), played a leading part in the unification of the states of the German Confederation into a German empire.

The first film was shown in Paris in 1895. The motion-picture camera and projector were invented by brothers Auguste and Louis Lumière.

When the Eiffel Tower was built in Paris as the entrance to the International Exhibition of 1889, it was the highest structure in the world.

The northern and southern states of America fought the Civil War from 1861 until 1865 during Abraham Lincoln's presidency. After victory by the northern army in 1865, slavery was abolished in the United States.

World-renowned Dutch painter Vincent van Gogh had little success in his lifetime.

People began experimenting with photographic techniques.

Carl Benz made the first car in 1885.

The 1900s were named the Belle Epoque or the Beautiful Era. In Paris the cancan was performed at the Moulin Rouge cabaret.

Henry Ford built an automobile empire using the assembly line technique of mass production. His Ford Model T car, first built in 1908, was immensely popular.

Europeans looked for a better future in the United States, Australia, Canada, and New Zealand. Steam ships such as the Titanic were specially designed for the ocean crossings.

European powers vied to colonize as much of Africa as possible.

The Belgian king Leopold II founded the Congo Free State as his own private property in 1885. His reign of terror caused the deaths of millions of indigenous people.

Using Zeppelins—airships filled with gas—the Germans bombed many European cities.

The opening shot of World War I was fired in Sarajevo on June 28, 1914. Archduke Franz Ferdinand was assassinated.

Because the Front barely moved, the soldiers dug themselves in. Much of World War I was fought from these trenches.

In 1914 the Germans wanted to march through Belgium to France. But the Belgians opened the sluices at Nieuwpoort and flooded the lowlands of the Yser River. The Germans could not advance, and the Front stayed in the same place for four years.

The British used their navy to blockade all supplies to Germany, which responded with submarine warfare. The Germans also torpedoed neutral ships, such as the Lusitania, which had many Americans on board—one of the reasons the Americans entered the war in 1917.

World War I

1914–1918

Prior to World War I, European countries had bound themselves together through mutual treaties. If one country was attacked, its allies agreed to come to its aid. In June 1914 a Serbian nationalist assassinated the successor to the Austrian throne, and Austria–Hungary declared war on Serbia, supported by its allies, which included Germany. The war lasted four years and involved nearly the whole world. It was the first war fought using modern technology, such as tanks and planes.

The German fighter pilot Manfred von Richthofen was nicknamed the Red Baron because of his bright red aircraft. Baron von Richthofen brought down 80 Allied planes.
After the armistice of November 11, 1918, the treaty formally ending the war was signed in Versailles the following year.
Yperite was the poison gas first used at Ypres. It was also known as mus t a r d g a s.
Because of the poem "In Flanders Fields," by Canadian John McCrae, the poppy became the symbol of World War I. McCrae saw the flower (which thrives on disturbed ground) blooming among the graves of his fallen comrades.

The 1920s

The miseries of war were followed by the "roaring twenties." The United States came out of the war strengthened, and the country became ever more prosperous. Its influence on Europe increased. It was the time of jazz music and gangsters. The carefree years of the 1920s ended abruptly with the collapse of the New York stock market.

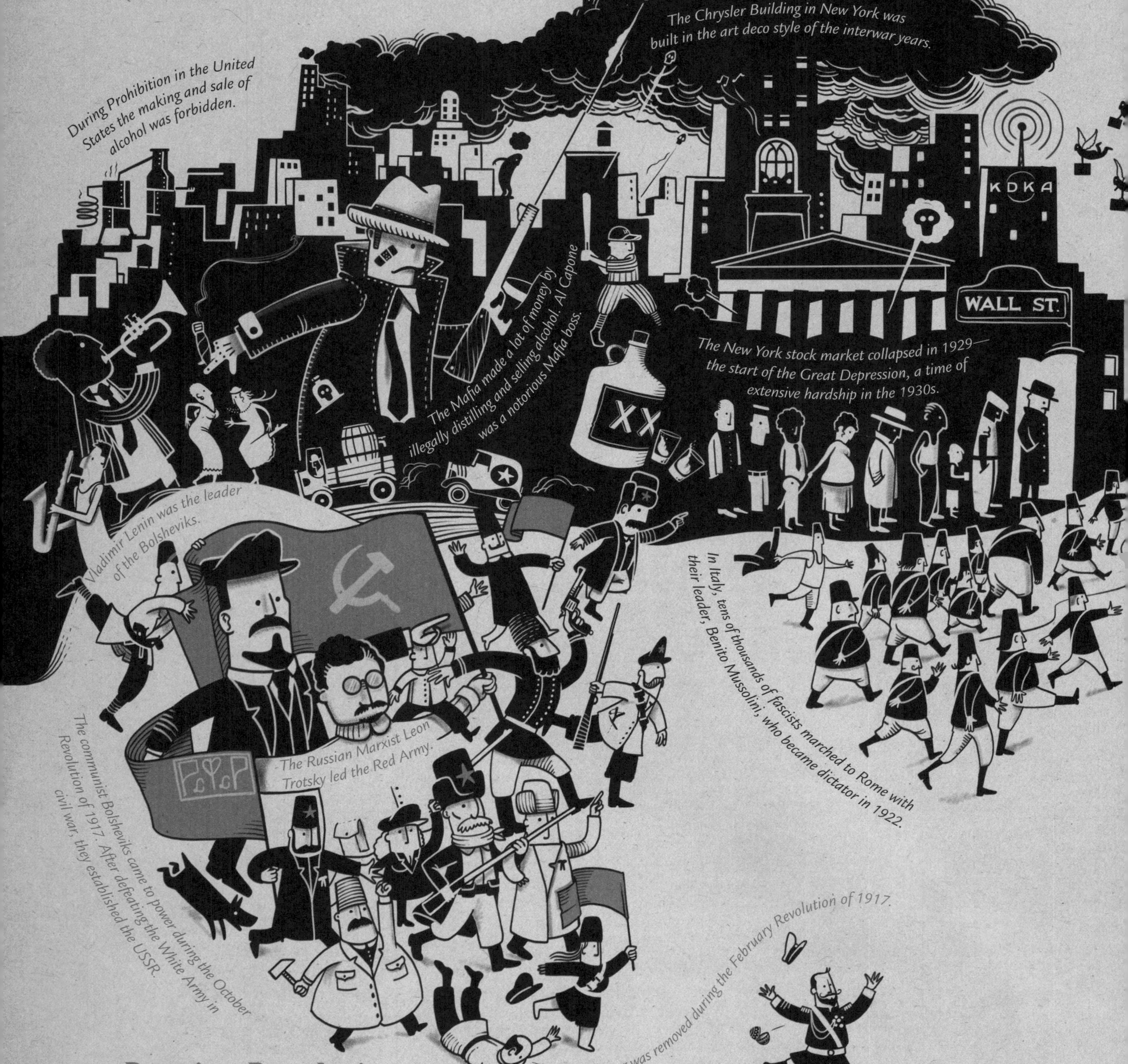
In 1922 insulin was used for the first time to treat a patient with diabetes.
Swimming champion Johnny Weissmuller starred in the Tarzan film of 1932.
The Chrysler Building in New York was built in the art deco style of the interwar years.
During Prohibition in the United States the making and sale of alcohol was forbidden.
KDKA
WALL ST.
The Mafia made a lot of money by illegally distilling and selling alcohol. Al Capone was a notorious Mafia boss.
The New York stock market collapsed in 1929—the start of the Great Depression, a time of extensive hardship in the 1930s.
XX
Vladimir Lenin was the leader of the Bolsheviks.
In Italy, tens of thousands of fascists marched to Rome with their leader, Benito Mussolini, who became dictator in 1922.
The Russian Marxist Leon Trotsky led the Red Army.
The communist Bolsheviks came to power during the October Revolution of 1917. After defeating the White Army in civil war, they established the USSR.
The Russian tsar was removed during the February Revolution of 1917.

The Russian Revolution

For centuries the Russian tsar virtually ruled supreme. But the empire was so extensive that it was difficult to govern. Most of the population lived in poverty, isolated in the countryside, and there was a wide gap between the poor and the sophisticated Westernized nobility. In 1917, when Russia looked to be no match for the German army, the tsar was deposed. Following a struggle for power among the insurgents, the communists won. They radically overturned the whole of Russian society. The USSR, or the Soviet Union, was born.

The 1930s

In the United States, the financial crash of 1929 led to the Great Depression of the 1930s; jobs and food became scarce, worsened by drought in farming areas. The Depression's effects were felt in Europe. Germany was crippled by the huge reparations (penalties) it was required to pay after World War I. Discontent among the people made it easy for the National Socialist German Workers' (Nazi) Party to take power. Under their leader Adolf Hitler, the Nazis blamed the Jewish people for Germany's woes. A new war threatened.

In 1932 Amelia Earhart became the first woman to fly solo over the Atlantic Ocean.
Nobody wanted to travel by Zeppelin after the Hindenburg caught fire in midair and crashed in 1937.
Hindenburg
Of Mice and Men by John Steinbeck was published in 1937.
The Wizard of Oz by L. Frank Baum was made into a film in 1939.
The German Nazi Party came to power in 1933, led by Adolf Hitler.
er a nonviolent revolution in 1932, Phibun Songkhram became premier of Thailand.
The genius Albert Einstein proposed the special theory of relativity. Of Jewish descent, he was denounced by the Nazis and left Germany forever for the United States in the early 1930s.
Penicilline
Charlie CHAPLIN in MODERN TIMES
he British microbiologist Alexander Fleming discovered nicillin in 1928, revolutionising the treatment of infections.
Black athlete Jesse Owens won four gold medals for the United States at the 1936 Berlin Olympic Games. This did not fit with the racist ideology of the Nazis.
ickey Mouse appeared on screen in 1928. Steamboat Willie, de by Walt Disney, was the first cartoon with a soundtrack.
The Spanish Civil War between the Republican government and the Nationalist rebels was won by the rebels. The dictator General Francisco Franco led Spain from 1939 until his death in 1975.

Franklin Roosevelt was 32nd president of the United States from 1933 until his death in 1945.
Harry S. Truman was vice president in early 1945, and president from April 1945 until 1953.
Blitzkrieg is German
“lightning war.” The
invasion was carried
lightning speed.
Jewish girl Anne Frank wrote her world-famous diary in Amsterdam while hiding from the Nazis. She was discovered and sent to a concentration camp.
“Operation Overlord” was the codename for a military action designed to defeat Germany. Allied troops landed in Normandy on the French coast on June 6, 1944. This day, known as “D-Day,” began the liberation of occupied Europe.
The Germans had a secret weapon: flying bombs. The V1 was the first crewless jet aircraft in the world.
The Spitfire was a British fighter plane.
Winston Churchill was prime minister of Great Britain during World War II, then again between 1951 and 1955.

World War II 1939–1945

By the late 1930s the key Axis powers—which included Germany, Italy, and Japan—were rapidly building armies and wanting to expand. When Germany invaded Poland in 1939 in search of Lebensraum ("living space"), war was inevitable. Against the Axis were ranged the Allies, among them Britain, France, Canada, Poland, Australia, New Zealand, most of Scandinavia, and (from 1941) the United States and Soviet Union. World War II would bring almost the entire globe into conflict, and see a terrible new weapon come into being.

In 1938 Germany annexed Austria. The following year Germany occupied part of what was then Czechoslovakia.
Joseph Stalin ruled the Soviet Union from the 1920s until his death in 1953. He led a reign of terror.
Stalin and Hitler had signed a pact of non-aggression. But after Germany invaded the Soviet Union in 1941, the two countries were at war. Thousands would die on the Eastern Front.
The Battle of the Ardennes (1944)
Adolf Hitler was the leader of Nazi Germany from 1933 until he committed suicide in 1945.
When Hitler's armies invaded Poland in 1939, Great Britain and France declared war on Germany.
About six million Jews died in the German concentration and extermination camps. This became known as the Holocaust.
Benito Mussolini, the dictator of Italy, sided with Hitler.
The North African front stretched from Morocco to Egypt.
he Allies landed on Sicily in 1943 and defeated Mussolini.
Emperor Hirohito ruled Japan from 1926 until his death in 1989.
Hiroshima was destroyed in 1945 by the atomic bomb. Japan surrendered shortly afterward.
Japan was, like Italy, an ally of Germany. In 1941 it attacked the American naval base at Pearl Harbor, drawing the United States into World War II.

Under the leadership of Mahatma Gandhi, India achieved independence from Great Britain through nonviolent resistance. Gandhi was assassinated in 1948.
India became independent in 1947.
ERP
With the Marshall Plan, the United States agreed to help the European economy recover after the war.
Many Jews had fled to Palestine. The independent state of Israel was declared in 1948.
During the Nuremberg Trials in 1945, 20 high-ranking Nazis were tried for war crimes.
Following a civil war between nationalists and communists, the communist People's Republic of China was declared in 1949.
The Korean War broke out in 1950, during the Cold War period. It w
a conflict between communist North Korea and the Westernized South Kor
An armistice followed after three years, but the tension still simmers.
In 1945, after the war, 51 countries founded the United Nations to work together for peace, security, and human rights.
In the Netherlands, dykes were breached in the winter of 1953. Floods killed nearly 2000 and left tens of thousands homeless.
The American submarine USS Nautilus, the first nuclear-powered submarine, was also the first vesse to travel beneath the North Pole (in 1958).

1945–1950

Following the war, Germany was divided in two to prevent it from becoming a powerful nation again. The eastern half became the German Democratic Republic, which was occupied by the Soviet Union. The western half became the Federal Republic of Germany, also known as West Germany, which was occupied by the Americans, French, and British. The military and political tension between the communist, totalitarian Soviet Union and its allies in the East and the capitalist, democratic West became known as the Cold War. Around the rest of the world, colonial territories strived for independence.

1953 New Zealander Edmund Hillary and
alese Sherpa Tenzing Norgay were the first
to reach the summit of Mount Everest.
Paperbacks became very popular.
During the Cold War an armed truce existed between the Eastern Bloc and the West. It was a golden age for spies.
The Atomium was built for the International Exhibition in Brussels in 1958, the first major international exhibition since the war.
Iron Curtain was a border between the
munist Eastern Bloc and the capitalist
t. It was safeguarded by barbed
wire and mines.
The Warsaw Pact was a military alliance between communist countries in Eastern Europe. The pact was sealed in 1955 and dissolved in 1991.
James Dean played the role of Jim Stark in the American movie Rebel Without a Cause.
Fidel Castro took control of Cuba in 1959 and turned it into a socialist state.
Charles de Gaulle, who had proved himself during the two world wars, became president of France in 1959.
A new type of music emerged from the United States: rock 'n' roll.
American actor Marilyn Monroe was the sex symbol of the 1950s.
ere was one song on each side of a single, or 45-rpm record.
The Suez Crisis of 1956, a conflict about access to the Suez Canal (which separated Asia and Africa), led to war. On one side was Egypt; on the other the alliance of Israel, Great Britain, and France.

The 1950s

After World War II ended, reconstruction began and people's lives slowly improved. With help from the United States, Western Europe (including West Germany) recovered. Rapidly growing prosperity ensured the arrival of all sorts of new consumer technology, such as refrigerators, irons, and reliable cars. But the Cold War also caused anxiety.

The television series Star Trek first aired in
NCC-1701
The chimpanzee Ham was launched into space by the Americans in 1961.
Laika was a Russian dog that orbited Earth in a rocket launched on November 3, 1957.
Cosmonauts are Russian astronauts. Yuri Gagarin was the first person in space.
CCCP
The Americans sent their first satellite, Explorer 1, into space on February 1, 1958.
The Russians initiated the Space Race when they launched Sputnik 1 on October 4, 1957.
The Russian space station, Mir, was in service from 1986 until 2001. One meaning of Mir is "peace."
Telstar 1, the first communication satellite, was launched in 1962.
The International Space Station has orbited Earth since 1998.
The Hubble Space Telescope was launched in 1990.
Crewless space probes, such as Voyager 1 and 2 and New Horizons, have been sent to explore the most distant planets in our solar system.
The American Pioneer program sends crewless probes to the furthest reaches of the solar system.

Americans and Russians worked together on the Apollo–Soyuz test project. In 1975 a Russian and an American space capsule docked in orbit.
In 1997 a robotic spacecraft, the Mars Pathfinder, took measurements on the red planet.
The Mars Science Laboratory, also known as Curiosity, is a crewless craft.
The animated series Futurama showed from 1999 until 2013.
Eight space shuttles were in use between 1981 and 2011.
The Mariner 9 was the first satellite to orbit Mars, from 1971 until 1972.
During a spacewalk the astronaut or cosmonaut floats free of gravity.
a gas giant with conspicuous rings.
The Orion spacecraft made its first flight in 2014.
The American Neil Armstrong was the first person to set foot on the moon, on July 21, 1969.

Space travel

During the Cold War, space exploration became an area of fervent competition between the Soviet Union and the United States. Their motives were mainly military, but the scientific community gained greatly as well. At first they experimented with crewless craft. Later, animals were sent into space. The first person in space was a Russian, but the first person on the moon was an American. Because Mars is much further away from Earth than the moon, it has not yet been reached, though missions are being planned. In the meantime, crewless vehicles gather data about the red planet.

The Argentinean Che Guevara led the guerrilla forces in the Cuban Revolution. After his violent death in 1967 he became an icon of Marxism.
Cuban leader Fidel Castro is said to have survived 638 attempts on his life.
Cuban exiles failed in their attempt to invade the Bay of Pigs in 1961.
Four young men from Liverpool, England, becam world famous as the pop group The Beatles.
Artist Andy Warhol was a leading figure in the pop art movement, which elevated everyday objects to "art." Warhol painted 32 variations of a can of Campbell's soup.
Campbell's
CONDENSED
TOMATO
SOUP
The black religious leader Martin Luther King Jr. was assassinated in Memphis in 1968.
Despite the abolition of slavery, black Americans remained second-class citizens. The civil rights movement fought for equal rights.
Christiaan Barnard carried out the first heart transplant operat in South Africa on December 3, 1967.
On November 22, 1963, a sniper killed American president John F. Kennedy in Dallas.
There were huge street protests against the Vietnam War.
A music festival called Woodstock took place in the United States in 1969. It was a celebration of youth culture and "flower power."
MP
From 1955 until 1975 the United States fought against communism in Vietnam.
The Viet Cong were guerrilla fighters skilled at jungle camoufla

The 1960s

A counterculture developed following the rapid economic growth of the 1950s. Young people were no longer satisfied with working and earning money. Hippies grew out their hair and experimented with drugs, clashing with conventional consumerist society. Many were opposed to the Vietnam War, and demonstrations for peace and social equality were widespread.

The first James Bond film came out in 1962.

During the time of the Berlin Wall, around 5000 people from East Berlin fled to the West.

After World War II, Berlin was divided into communist East Berlin and capitalist West Berlin. In 1961 the communists built the Berlin Wall as part of the Iron Curtain. The wall remained in place until 1989.

In 1968 Czechoslovakia wanted more freedom. But Soviet tanks quickly brought an end to the "Prague Spring."

YOU ARE LEAVING
THE AMERICAN SECTOR
ВЫ ВЫЕЗЖАЕТЕ ИЗ
АМЕРИКАНСКОГО СЕКТОРА
VOUS SORTEZ
DU SECTEUR AMÉRICAIN
SIE VERLASSEN DEN AMERIKANISCHEN SEKTOR

POLICE

Workers in Paris went on strike in May 1968, supported by students. The uprising became known as "May 68."

BRITS OUT

I.R.A

The Belgian Eddy Merckx won the Tour de France several times.

"The Troubles" in Northern Ireland was a period of unrest and violence from the late 1960s until 1998.

Mao Zedong wrote the Little Red Book. As leader of the People's Republic of China, he was known as the Great Helmsman. He set in motion the Cultural Revolution (1966–1976) in the last decade of his life.

Between 1966 and 1996, 210 nuclear tests were carried out in French Polynesia by the French military.

When America supported Israel in the Yom Kippur War, Arab countries chose to stop supplying oil to Western countries and Japan. This prompted the oil crisis of 1973.
Many European countries instituted car-free Sundays to conserve scarce fuel supplies.
The price of gas rose by 70 percent.
PREMIUM
The Carnation Revolution brought democracy to Portugal in 1974.
American director Steven Spielberg released the film Jaws in 1975.
Helped by the United States, General Pinochet of Chile led a coup in 1973.
American president Richard Nixon resigned in 1974 as a result of the Watergate scandal.
The world's first email was sent in 1971 over the ARPANET, the forerunner of the Internet.
In 1973 an Egyptian–Syrian coalition attacked Israel on the Jewish holy day of Yom Kippur starting the Yom Kippur War.
Pong was one of the first video games.
Palestinian terrorists took Israeli athletes hostage at the Munich Olympic Games in 1972. All nine athletes died.
The Ugandan dictator Idi Amin took power in 1971. More than 300 000 people died during his reign.
The secret informant who leaked information about the Watergate scandal to journalists used the pseudonym Deep Throat.
Land art is art rooted in the landscape. In 1970 the American artist Robert Smithson created Spiral Jetty, a pier in the shape of a spiral.
The cod wars were a series of disputes between Britain and Iceland running from the 1950s to the 1970s over the rights to fish in Icelandic waters.

Industrial computer-controlled robots accomplished complicated tasks on the assembly line.
Steve Jobs and Steve Wozniak founded the computer company Apple in 1976.
Bill Gates and Paul Allen started Microsoft in 1975.
The communist party seized power in Afghanistan in 1978. The Mujahideen (Islamic resistance fighters) rose up in opposition. The Soviet Union sent troops to help the communists.
The Shah of Iran, who was following Western ideas, was deposed in 1979. The Muslim cleric, or ayatollah, Ruhollah Khomeini came to power.
The Australian rock band AC/DC released their first album in 1975.
In 1978 the Camp David Accords saw Egypt recognize the right of Israel to exist.
As well as a musical style, punk was a way of life and a fashion statement.
Margaret Thatcher was prime minister of the United Kingdom from 1979 to 1990. She was nicknamed the Iron Lady.
The communist Khmer Rouge waged a war of terror in Cambodia. One-quarter of the population died. An invasion by the Vietnamese ended the slaughter.
China's one-child policy was designed to curb population growth.

The 1970s

Hippie fashions included wide flares, vivid hues, and striking patterns. Natural fabrics were increasingly replaced by synthetics. Nearly everyone had a car. In the Middle East the conflict between Israel and the Arab world continued to simmer. As a consequence, the price of gasoline rocketed. Because of the political tension between the Arab world and the West, in 1973 the Arab countries instigated an oil embargo. This prompted the 1973 oil crisis.

HIV, a new and frightening virus which can lead to AIDS, appeared in the early 1980s.

The computer game Pac-Man came out in 1980.

Iraq and Iran were at war from 1980 until 1998.

In 1982 Steven Spielberg made the film ET, about an alien who wants to go home.

In 1984 British mine workers were on strike for nearly a year in protest against the closing of state mines.

COAL NOT DOLE

COAL NOT DOLE

The CCC—a communist terrorist organization—and the Brabant killers spread terror in Belgium.

Strikes broke out all over Poland, heralding the end of the communist regime. Lech Wałęsa formed Solidarity, the first trade union in a communist country. He later became president of Poland and received the Nobel Peace Prize.

The president of the Soviet Union, Mikhail Gorbachev, introduced glasnost ("openness") and perestroika ("restructuring"). These measures led to the end of the Cold War and, indirectly, to the end of the Soviet Republic. In 1990 Gorbachev received the Nobel Peace Prize.

SOLIDARNOŚĆ

Rubik's cube, a puzzle, was all the rage.

MIX TAPE

Cassettes gave people a way to make mix tapes or compilations. They got a new lease of life after the launch of the Sony Walkman in 1979.

Prince Charles of England married Diana Spencer in 1981. They divorced 10 years later.

MTV began broadcasting music videos in 1981.

Michael Jackson, the King of Pop

In 1982 Argentina and the United Kingdom fought over the Falklands, a group of islands at the southern tip of South America. The Falklands War was won by the United Kingdom.

In 1986, at Chernobyl in Ukraine—then part of the Soviet Union—a nuclear reactor exploded with disastrous consequences for the environment and local people.
The Berlin Wall fell in 1989, then the rest of the Iron Curtain crumbled. One by one, communist regimes toppled or allowed democratic elections.
Music could be played anywhere with a boombox.
The first PCs, or personal computers, appeared.
LIVE AID
Live Aid, a benefit concert for famine relief in Ethiopia, was held in 1985.
In 1988 Libyan terrorists brought down an American airliner over Lockerbie, Scotland.
Student-led protests for economic and political reform, held in Tiananmen Square in China in 1989, were met with a violent crackdown by the Chinese military.
The video game Tetris could be played on the Game Boy, released in 1989.
Nintendo GAME BOY
A DeLorean car became a time machine in the 1985 film Back to the Future.
e shipwreck of the oil tanker Exxon Valdez
n 1989 caused an environmental disaster.

The 1980s

The early 1980s saw the nuclear arms race grow ever more tense between the superpowers of the United States and USSR, but the decade's end brought an unexpected and dramatic change. The communist Eastern Bloc collapsed and the Berlin Wall came down—the Cold War was over. New technologies advanced unchecked, and more and more people bought home computers. The disaster at Chernobyl showed how dangerous a nuclear power station could be.

The Maastricht Treaty, which created the European Union, was signed in 1992.

Under Saddam Hussein, Iraq invaded Kuwait, starting the Gulf War (1990–1991).

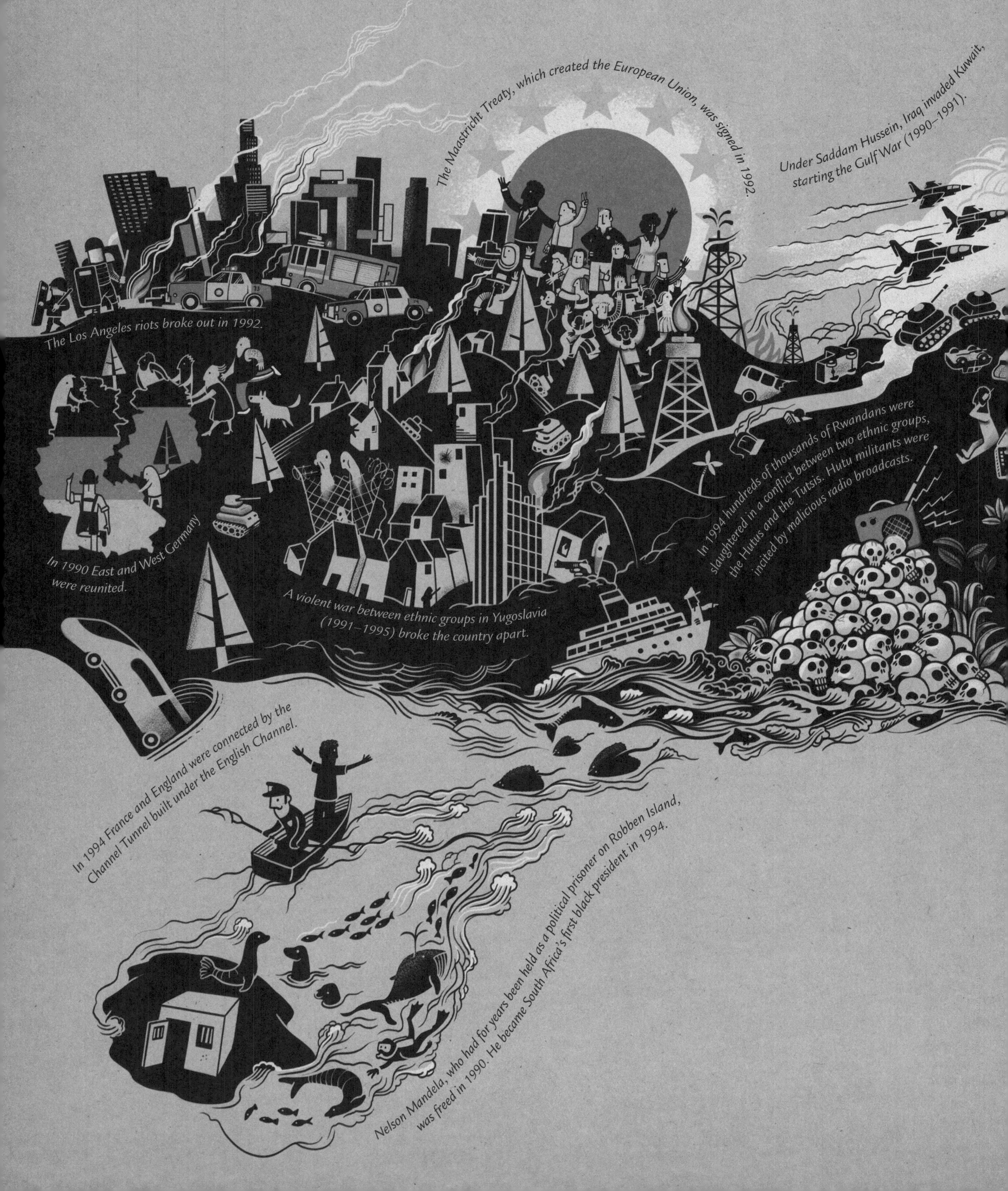

The Los Angeles riots broke out in 1992.

In 1994 hundreds of thousands of Rwandans were slaughtered in a conflict between two ethnic groups, the Hutus and the Tutsis. Hutu militants were incited by malicious radio broadcasts.

In 1990 East and West Germany were reunited.

A violent war between ethnic groups in Yugoslavia (1991–1995) broke the country apart.

In 1994 France and England were connected by the Channel Tunnel built under the English Channel.

Nelson Mandela, who had for years been held as a political prisoner on Robben Island, was freed in 1990. He became South Africa's first black president in 1994.

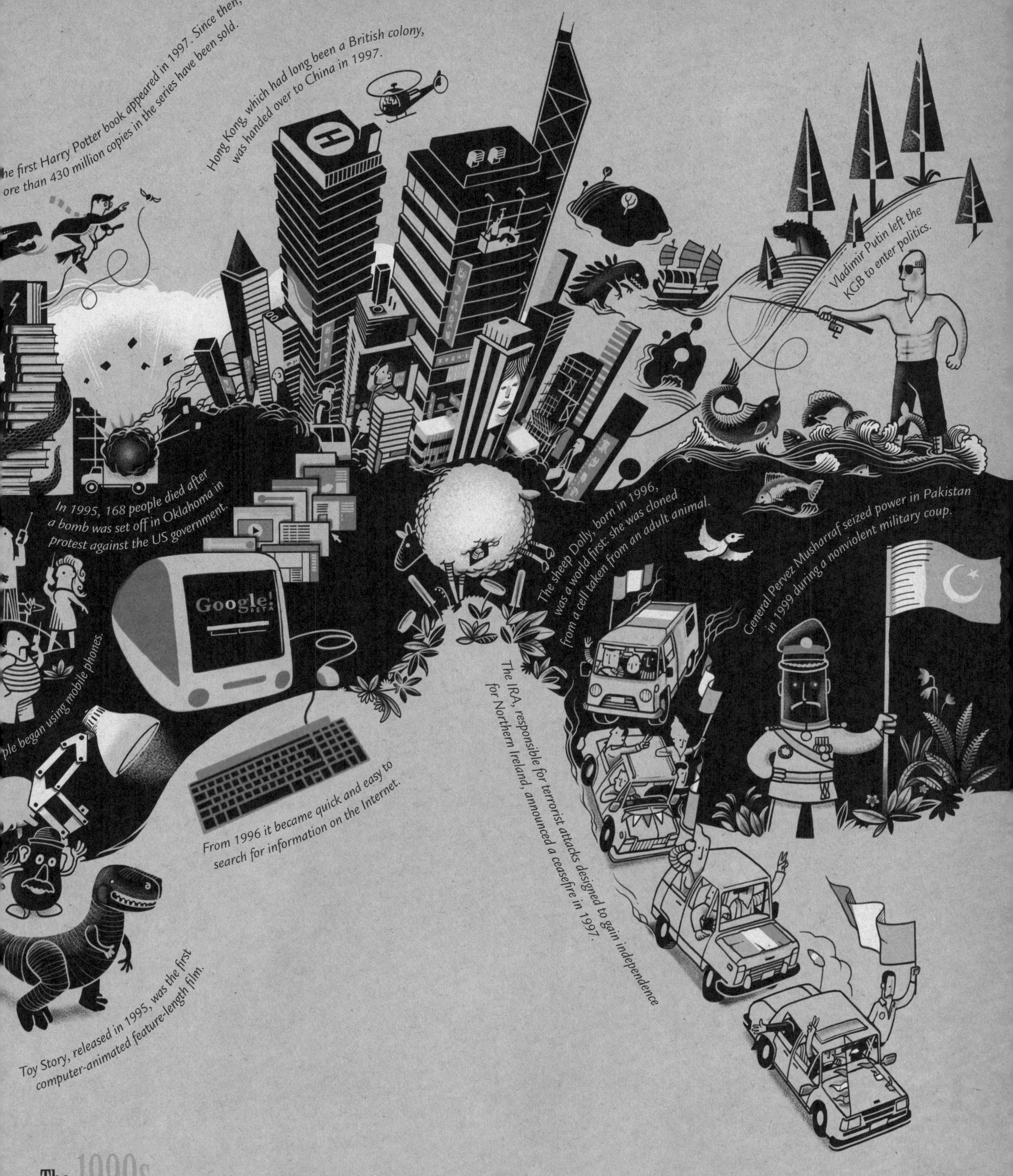
he first Harry Potter book appeared in 1997. Since then,
ore than 430 million copies in the series have been sold.
Hong Kong, which had long been a British colony, was handed over to China in 1997.
Vladimir Putin left the KGB to enter politics.
In 1995, 168 people died after a bomb was set off in Oklahoma in protest against the US government.
Google!
The sheep Dolly, born in 1996, was a world first: she was cloned from a cell taken from an adult animal.
General Pervez Musharraf seized power in Pakistan in 1999 during a nonviolent military coup.
ple began using mobile phones.
From 1996 it became quick and easy to search for information on the Internet.
The IRA, responsible for terrorist attacks designed to gain independence for Northern Ireland, announced a ceasefire in 1997.
Toy Story, released in 1995, was the first computer-animated feature-length film.

The 1990s

As computers grew ever more powerful, appearing in more and more offices and homes, the Internet and mobile phones changed the world. Scientists experimented further with the creation of life. But conflict rumbled on. Ethnic violence raged in Africa, and also in the former Yugoslavia. And in the Middle East, Saddam Hussein unleashed a war that involved the Western world.

On September 11, 2001, two hijacked passenger aircraft plunged into the skyscrapers of the World Trade Center in New York. Responsibility for the attack was claimed by Islamic terrorist group Al Qaeda.

On December 26, 2004, an undersea earthquake in the Indian Ocean unleashed a massive tsunami, causing one of the worst-ever natural disasters.

War in Darfur, Sudan, lasted from 2003 to 2010. The conflict between Arab and non-Arab groups was about water and land.

As a result of 9/11, the United States and its allies waged war in Afghanistan from 2001 until 2012.

In 2003 the United States and its allies invaded Iraq seeking to bring down the regime of Saddam Hussein.

Euro notes and coins were introduced across Europe in 2002.

British professor J.R.R. Tolkien wrote The Lord of the Rings in the 1940s. In 2001 director Peter Jackson filmed the first part of the trilogy.

Banksy is a British graffiti artist. No one knows for sure who he really is.

Mark Zuckerberg founded Facebook in 2004.

Hurricane Katrina flooded the American city of New Orleans in 2005.

2008 the United States elected its first
black president, Barack Obama.
The Arab Spring—a wave of demonstrations and revolution in North
Africa and the Middle East—began in Tunisia in 2010.
Incandescent light bulbs were banned
from sale in Europe from 2009 as a
measure to save energy.
Angela Merkel became chancellor
of Germany in 2005.
Social media became increasingly popular.
You Tube
People swapped their ordinary
mobile phones for smartphones.
n Rompuy became the first president of the European Union.
FOR SALE
SALE
The website WikiLeaks, set up in 2006, made public
secret information from anonymous sources.
London was rocked by terrorist attacks
the morning rush hour.
A credit crisis started in the United States in 2007 with the
collapse of the housing market. The effects were felt worldwide.
An explosion on an oil platform in the Gulf of Mexico
in 2010 caused an environmental disaster.
For three months, oil leaked into the sea.

The 2000s

As a new millennium dawned, many feared that a bug would crash the world's computers. Luckily, their fears were unfounded. But the 2000s would see huge changes across society. Suicide attacks on New York City and Washington, D.C., caused the death of nearly 3000 people and widened the gap between the Western and Arab worlds. Natural disasters, too, took their toll, and later in the decade the credit crisis sent unemployment levels rocketing. At the end of the decade, the Arab Spring brought hope for change in North Africa and the Middle East. And technological change continued apace: Facebook conquered the world, and the mobile phone became our constant companion.

The 2010s

Terrorism. Conflict. Eco-disasters. You'd think the world would have changed by now, but maybe not. Environmental concerns and the fight against terrorism make the news headlines. Wars and poverty bring streams of refugees to Europe, with thousands risking their lives in unseaworthy boats in search of a better life. Yes, Europeans scrambled out of economic crisis, and we have untold computing power in our pocket—but peace and prosperity for all remains a distant dream.

In 2014 the passenger airliner MH17 was shot down near the Russia–Ukraine border. All the passengers, most of whom were Dutch or Malaysian, died.
An earthquake at sea damaged the nuclear power plant at Fukushima in Japan with disastrous consequences.
Data was increasingly stored in the "cloud."
The self-named Islamic State was responsible for cruelty and brutal violations of human rights.
Pharrell Williams's song "Happy" was a hit in 2013.
The Belgians took 541 days to form a government—a new record.
The first 3-D printers for home use came onto the market.
As time goes by...
The construction of wind turbines increas in the search for renewable energy.
JE SUIS CHARLIE
JE SUIS CHARLIE
Will the electric car soon become common?
The cruise ship Costa Concordia capsized in 2012 off the Italian coast.
On January 7, 2015, 12 people were shot dead by Muslim extremists after the French magazine Charlie Hebdo published cartoons of the prophet Mohammed. People massed on the streets to defend freedom of speech.
Refugees in boats attempted to enter Europe via the Mediterranean Sea. Many boats capsized because they were unsafe and overloaded.

Thanks to Fien Danniau, Christophe Verbruggen, and Tom De Paepe, and to the Lannoo team: Sofie, Wendy, and Judith

www.petergoes.com
www.facebook.com/petergoesillustrator

This edition first published in 2015 by Gecko Press
PO Box 9335, Marion Square, Wellington 6141, New Zealand
info@geckopress.com

First American edition published in 2016 by Gecko Press USA, an imprint of Gecko Press Ltd

Original title: *Tijdlijn*. Translated from the Dutch language.
2015 © Uitgeverij Lannoo nv.
www.lannoo.com

Distributed in the United States and Canada by Lerner Publishing Group, www.lernerbooks.com
Distributed in the United Kingdom by Bounce Sales and Marketing, www.bouncemarketing.co.uk
Distributed in Australia by Scholastic Australia, www.scholastic.com.au
Distributed in New Zealand by Upstart Distribution, www.upstartpress.co.nz

The translation of this book was funded by the Flemish Literature Fund
www.flemishliterature.be

Flemish Literature Fund

Rubik's Cube® used by permission Rubik's Brand Ltd www.rubiks.com

Text by Peter Goes and Sylvia Vanden Heede
Translated by Bill Nagelkerke
Typesetting by Vida & Luke Kelly, New Zealand
Printed in Slovakia

ISBN: 978-1-776570-69-0

For more curiously good books, visit www.geckopress.com

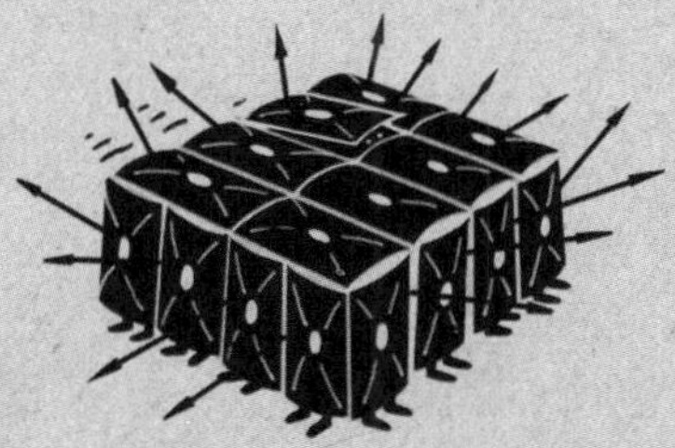

PETER GOES

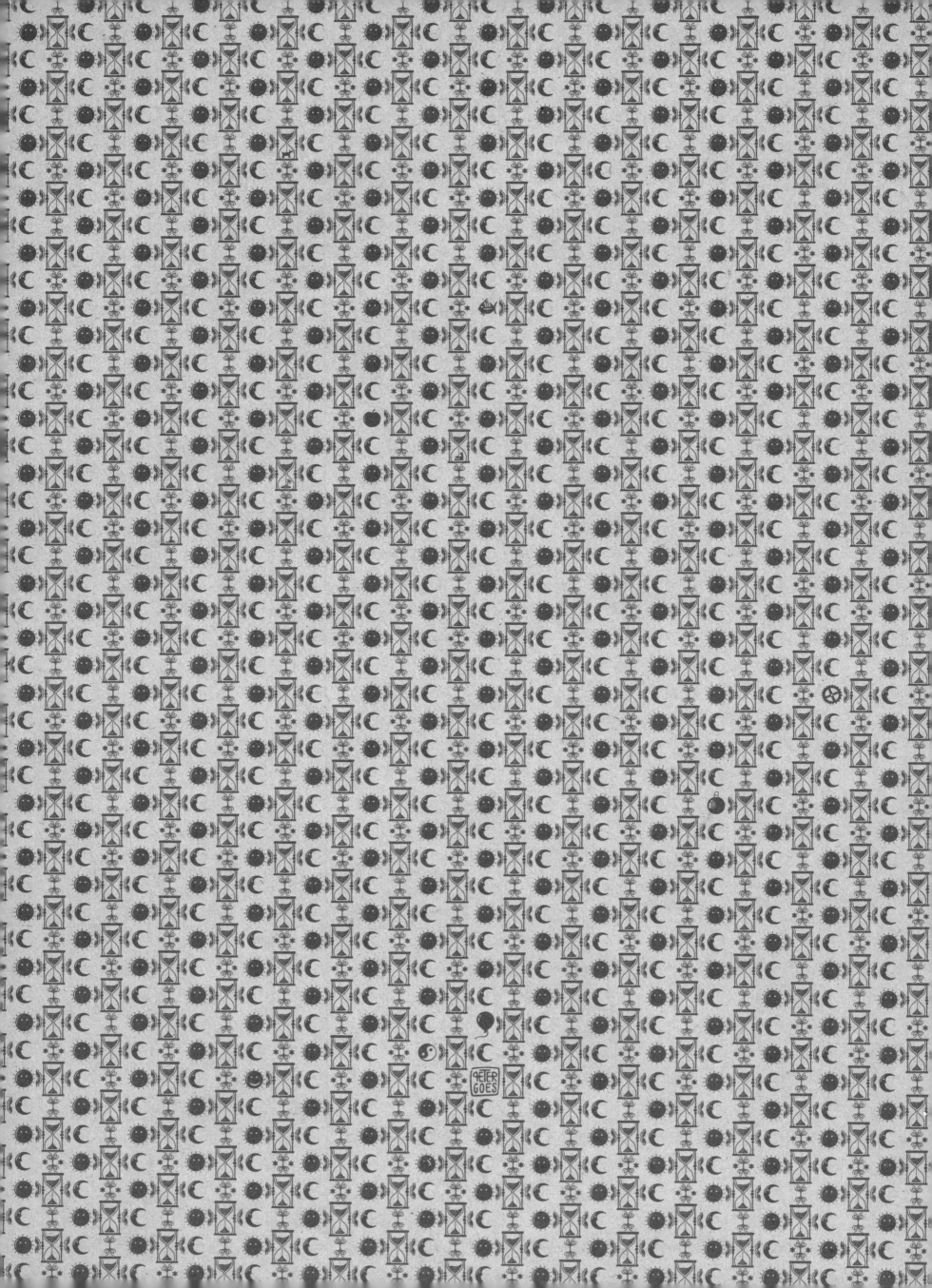